Fletchery!

The Art of Making Matched Arrows

by Bill Searle

2011

Dyfi Valley Bookshop

Machynlleth

First published in 2000 by
Bill Searle

This edition published 2011 by
The Dyfi Valley Bookshop
6 Doll Street, Machynlleth,
Powys, SY20 8BQ

ISBN 978-1463684037

Covers designed by Neil Beeby

Contents

Introduction.

So you want to make yourself a set of arrows to match your bow, which will group in the gold at every end? Don't we all?

I can't guarantee that, but I will show you how to provide yourself with a set of eight or more self arrows, which will be matched within the following limits: -

+/- 5 grains in weight.
+/- 1 G.N.A.S (Grand National Archery Society) unit in spine.
+/- ¼ inch in point of balance.

Later on, I will show you how to make the "non plus ultra" of target arrows – a rosewood footed, barrelled arrow of the best quality.

Why matched arrows? – Would you consider shooting anything but arrows from a matched set in your recurve bow? Matched to each other, and just as importantly, matched to the bow! With a recurve you are shooting your arrow much nearer to the centre line of the bow, and under these conditions the archer's paradox has less effect. With a longbow the arrow is much further off the bow's centre line. Arrow spine is important, and spine matching, both to the other arrows in the set and to the bow, is vital, if you are to attain good groups.

To make these arrows, you will need, apart from a few hand tools, three things: -

1. A balance, capable of weighing up to 500 grains to an accuracy of 1 grain.
2. A spine tester, capable of measuring spine to 1 G.N.A.S unit.
3. A supply of suitable timber from which to make your arrows.

Do not despair! Both the balance and the spine tester are not difficult to make and I will show you how. The arrow shafts which you can buy from archery dealers, spined as they are by the American method and not weighed, are generally speaking, not good enough to make a matched set of arrows to the specification above. I will tell you how to obtain the necessary timber and how to work it.

But first of all, for those of you who are not familiar with it, a short explanation of the "Archers Paradox" and its relation to arrow spine and the matching of arrows.

The Archers Paradox.

When you nock an arrow on the string of your longbow, if you are right handed, you will find the arrow pointing far to the left. This is due of course to the width of the bow at the arrow plate. Why then does your arrow, if it is correctly matched to the bow, behave when loosed as if it had been shot through the centre line of the bow? This is essentially the paradox as seen by longbow men down the ages, and it was not until the advent of high-speed photography that the mystery was solved. Briefly what happens is this: -

When the arrow is loosed at full draw, its first action (under the push of the string, and due to the inertia of the pile and other factors) is to bend inward, i.e., concave toward the bow. Its natural reaction is then to straighten out and then bend in the other direction. In other words, we have made the arrow vibrate, and depending on how "springy" the shaft is, it will continue to vibrate for some time after leaving the string. The vibrations will eventually reduce to zero. In order for the arrow to leave the bow cleanly, it must make 1½ cycles of its vibrations during the time taken to travel from the loose to the point where the feathers clear the bow. The stiffer the arrow is, the faster it will vibrate, so therefore a faster bow needs a stiffer arrow. Generally speaking, bow draw weight relates to speed – the heavier the draw weight, the faster the bow.

The Paradox

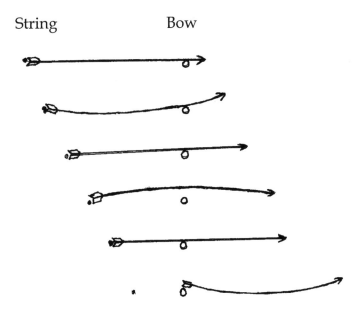

String   Bow

The stiffness of an arrow is measured on a "spine tester" in G.N.A.S units of spine, which are a measure of the deflection of the arrow in 1/100ths of an inch, under a weight of 1 ½ pounds. Obviously, a greater deflection equals a higher spine number, and therefore a "whippier" arrow.

Many archers shoot arrows which are too stiff (lower spine number) for their bows. An arrow that is too stiff will fly to the left for a right-handed archer, and may indeed hit the bow on release and "start", flying erratically, whereas a too whippy arrow may fly to the right. For a much too stiff arrow, look for marks on the shaft, just below, or between the shaft feathers.

It follows that for good arrow flight your arrows must be of the correct spine for your bow and also be of the same spine as each other to within one or two units. Here is a list of suggested arrow spines for various bow weights and arrow lengths. They may not be absolutely accurate for your particular bow, because your style of shooting, and especially your loose, will also have an effect on the behaviour of your arrows.

Draw Weight (lbs.)	Arrow Length (inches)		Spine (G.N.A.S. units)
25 (5'9" bow)	26		85
30 (5'9" bow)	26		80
35 (5'9" or 6' bow)	26	28	75
40		28	70
45		28	65
50		28	60
55		28	58
60		28	55

More information when we build the spine tester, but for now, on to timber. Both the balance and spine tester are detailed later.

Timber

A number of timbers are suitable for the manufacture of arrows. One of the best of these is Port Orford Cedar, which as far as I know is only obtainable in this country from archery dealers. It is sold in dowel form, and spined by the American method, whereby you can buy your shafts sorted into bow-weight categories, but un-weighed. If you want to make matched arrows this is not a practical proposition (as you will realise when you read the chapter on sorted dowels), unless you can persuade a dealer to allow you (armed with spine tester and balance) to sort through his stock.

Other perfectly good timbers are:- Redwood (pine), Douglas Fir, Sitka Spruce and Scots Pine. Of these, Redwood is probably the easiest to obtain. It is the timber most commonly used by joiners for construction work, flooring, cladding etc and is often (wrongly) called "Deal". Usually, it is knotty and anything but straight grained. However, if you are prepared to search, it is possible to find 36" lengths of knot free, straight and close-grained material. Most timber merchants will let you look through their stock of dressed timber if you explain what you need. You will probably move a lot of timber in your search. *If you want to be allowed to repeat the exercise next time you need wood, you must leave the timber in as neat or neater condition than you found it!*

You are looking for dressed timber, 3" x 2" (or equivalent i.e. 6" x 1") or greater, with a length of about 3 feet, knot free, straight and close grained. You will be sawing your timber into $^3/_8$" square sticks, which will be converted to $^{11}/_{32}$" dowels. From a piece of 3" x 2" you will get 24 sticks and you will almost certainly find eight or more $^{11}/_{32}$" dowels closely enough matched to make a set of arrows to the specifications above. Of course, the larger your piece of timber, the better your chances of matched dowels. You will probably have to buy the full length of timber that contains the piece you want, although some merchants will cut the section you need. Even so, it is still a cheap way to get a matched set of arrows.

Conversion to Dowels.

I use a band saw to convert my timber to $^3/_8''$ square sticks. There are three ways of converting the squares to $^{11}/_{32}''$ dowels.

Method 1.

You can lay your square stick in a groove machined in the edge of a plank, and with a *sharp*, fine-set plane, take off the corners to produce an eight sided figure. Keep planing off the corners until your dowel is circular. Then reduce it until it will *just* go through a $^{23}/_{64}''$ hole drilled in a piece of 1'' MDF (see chapter on jigs for description of hole size jig and also dowel plate). When you have it to this size, reduce it with 40-grit sandpaper on a block to $^{11}/_{32}''$.

If you have a dowel plate, you can, when the dowel is circular, hammer it through successively smaller holes in the plate, but not smaller than $^{23}/_{64}''$. At this size, use the coarse
sanding block to reduce your dowel to the final $^{11}/_{32}''$. *Whenever you are reducing timber, with either plane or sanding block, never plane or sand from end to end of your timber. If you do, you will almost certainly end up with a dowel which is thin in the middle. Always work from the centre to each end of your wood.*

Method 2.

The second method of reducing your sticks to dowels is with the "Ashem" rounding plane, an illustration of which is shown below but also see the chapter on tools.

The "Ashem" Rounding Plane

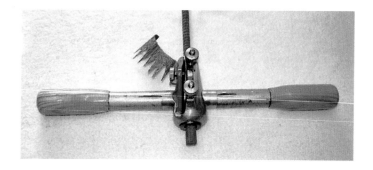

This requires that you feed the plane down a rotating square stick to produce a round dowel – hence "rounding plane". To this end, you need to drive the stick at something like 400 rpm. If you procure a piece of $^3/_8$" square metal, about 2" long and either turn or have turned 1" of one end down concentrically to about $^5/_{16}$" diameter, this will fit in the chuck of a pistol drill. You need to fix four "wings" to the square to form a hollow $^3/_8$" square, into which you can insert one end of your $^3/_8$" square stick. The drill, preferably a variable speed model, must be held horizontally in some kind of bench stand.

Put one end of your stick into the ½" entrance hole of the rounder, and the other end into your jig in the drill chuck. Start the drill, feed the rounder down the jig. Stop the drill, and cut off your dowel just clear of the exit hole of the rounder, and you have your first dowel.

A few hints and tips.

1. Keep the rounder blade *sharp* and well set up as per the manufacturers instructions.
2. Your stick should be a good fit in the entrance bush of the rounder. If it is too big, it will be hard work and your rounder will soon run hot. Two possible cures: - a) plane off the corners of the square, or b) make yourself a brass or steel bush with a ½" hole. Hold it in the vice and push (or hammer!) your stick through to take off the corners.
3. If you can arrange a foot switch to power your drill it leaves both hands free and makes life much easier.
4. If you start with 36" sticks, you will end up with about 32" dowels (you loose 4 to 4 ½ inches in the rounder). If you do not want arrows longer than say 28 inches, you can of course use shorter timber, *but make your dowels long enough!* You can always shorten them, but once cut, you cannot conveniently lengthen them.

ʏod 3.

ʏʜe third method of conversion is by the use of a jig adapted from one designed by Patrick Spielman, which is illustrated in his book "Router Jigs and Techniques". Fig 1 shows a general picture of the jig.

Fig 1.

The two pieces of hardwood of about $1^1/_2$ inches x ¾ inch x 12 inches long are clamped together and trimmed to exactly the same length. Whilst clamped together, a pilot hole is drilled through centre of the pair. The holes can be opened out to $^{11}/_{32}"$ for the hole marked "B" or ½" for hole "A". Alternatively, both holes may be opened out to take two brass bushes with $^{11}/_{32}"$ and ½" holes respectively. These two pieces are then joined together by bolting to the two pieces marked "C" which are shaped so that the original pieces are held 1" apart, allowing for the introduction of a router staff bead cutter (Axminster Power Tool Co., cat. no 800145 or equivalent). The two parts marked "C" are also drilled to take the router mounting rods, positioned so that the router just clears the frame, and also have a central hole to take a 6mm screwed rod. Two 6mm screwed rods are used to position the router so that the cutter is just in line with the $^{11}/_{32}"$ outlet shown in Fig 2.

Fig 2

The two adjusting wheels are circles of about 1 ½″ diameter MDF carrying inserted M6 nuts. These are shown in more detail in Fig 3.

Fig 3

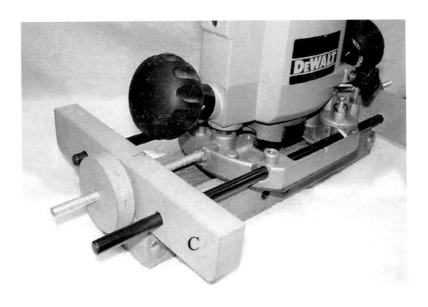

.djustment is critical and the dowel should come out polished, but must not run tight ugh to get hot.

In operation, the stick, held in the holder (Fig 4) is driven at fairly high speed and fed through the ½" hole in the frame, against the revolving router cutter (Fig 5).

Fig 4   **Fig 5**

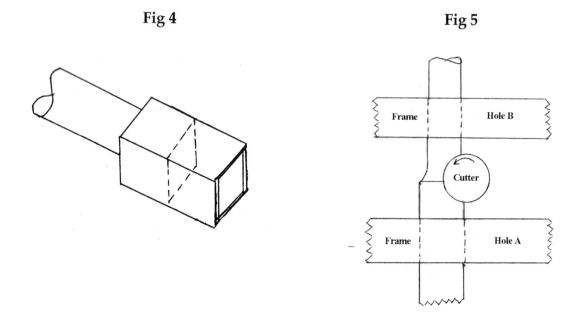

A 3/8" square stick is slightly over ½" corner to corner, so the ½" hole will just rub off the corners of the stick and keep it steady.

If you have cut your sticks slightly oversize, the make yourself a brass or steel bush with a ½" hole, and drive the stick through it first.

The holder shown in Fig 5 is made from a length of 3/8" square brass or "Dural" with a section turned down to fit into a drill chuck. Extensions are fitted to the other end to form a hollow square section, which will take the stick.

Notes.

1. I you want to make different sized dowels (say $^5/_{16}$" or $^9/_{32}$") you can make another set of holes of the required sizes, displaced from the original holes, and reposition the router accordingly.

2. Make your sticks 4 inches longer than the arrows you want, as you will lose about 1 inch at the start of your dowel and 2 to 3 inches at the end.

Sorting Dowels.

Your dowels should all be of the same length. If not, I will tell you later how to compensate. Sand any rough patches on your dowels until all are reasonably smooth. Now make sure they are straight. If not, they can be straightened by heating. A good source of heat is a hot air paint stripper, held in a "Workmate" at an angle pointing slightly upwards and away from you. Twirl the bent dowel in your fingers, directing the hot air to the bend, and then straighten. It takes practice but persevere!

You can now weigh and spine each dowel, writing the spine and weight on the end of each one as in Fig 6 below.

Fig 6

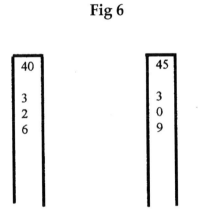

Spine all your dowels at the same length in accordance with the instructions given with the spine tester. 27" is a reasonable length, *but whatever length you use, use it always* and in future you can add to your stock with the knowledge that the spines are comparable.

A tip here with regard to weights: obviously you cannot compare weights of different length dowels directly. However, if you take the weight of a shorter dowel, divide by its' length and multiply by the length of the longer one, the two weights are directly comparable. For example: -

Dowel A = 28" and 300 grains
Dowel B = 32"

Comparable weight = 300 / 28 x 32 = 342 grains

you sort your dowels, your 28"/300 grain one will go in with the 340 to 350 group. you do this, it is a good idea to mark the shorter dowel (say with a "c") to denote that the weight is a comparable one. Now sort your dowels into weight bands of 10 grains, i.e. 310 to 320, 320 to 330, etc. With any bunch of dowels cut from the same piece of timber, you will probably find most in one or two bands, with less in the weight bands above and below these, and probably a spread of something like 10 units of spine. Depending on how many dowels you have, you should be able to find enough within 10 grains of weight and hopefully less than 10 units in spine to make a matched set of arrows, remembering than your weights do not have to be in one specific band. For example, your best set may be in two bands (say 315 to 325), but providing your set is within the 10-grain limit, you can get a good match.

Assume you have a set in the limits 315 to 325 and with spines of 50 to 57. If you find a dowel both heavy *and* stiff, say 48 spine and 330 grain, you will find it will make a match with the others. You can get a reasonable set with a band of 15 grains, or depending on spines, even 20 grains, but you may end up outside the +/- 5 grain weight specification.

For your first attempt, it is probably best to start with eight of your best match. Until you have had some practice, you will find it easier to juggle with eight rather than a dozen. Having said that, if you have a dozen well within the 10 grain limit and a spread of no more than 5 G.N.A.S units, go ahead with the lot!

You need a rack to hold your dowels while you work on them. Take a piece of 1 ½" x ¾" dressed timber, about 15" long and fit cross pieces at each end to act as feet, so that it will stand on edge. Drill $^{11}/_{32}$" holes on 1" centres and 1" deep along the edge. You should have at least 12. Number them from one end 1 to 12. These holes and numbers are the only identification your arrows will have while you are working on them, so only remove them one at a time and *never* have two out together. *If you get your shafts mixed up, the whole process becomes unworkable.* I cannot stress this too highly and I will remind you of it when we start to make arrows.

Making Arrows.

You must first decide your arrow length and the spine figure you want to achieve. Taking into account your bow draw weight, a list of suggested spine values for various bow/arrow combinations is given in the introduction.

One more task before we start. You must keep a record of all the work you do on each individual shaft. Make yourself a chart as Fig 7 below: -

Fig 7.

Initial Spec   *(number) 32" shafts*
42 - 47 spine at 27"
350 -356 grains

Additional Comments

Arrow Number	Spine	Weight
1		
2		
3		
4		
5		
etc		

Put this on a board and hang it somewhere convenient to your work. You will be using it a lot! Write on the top of your chart the spec of the shafts you are going to use. If you break an arrow in the future, you can replace it exactly if you find a new shaft within this spec.

Now put your shafts into the arrow rack in ascending order of weight. As mentioned earlier, only remove shafts one at a time to work on them. The numbers on the rack are your only means of identification and so on no account get your shafts mixed.

.r shafts are not of the correct length, remove them now, one at a time and cut to ‚th. You will later have to cut a little more off, because with a pile and nock fitted, ‚ ur arrow will have "grown" by about 1". With your shafts all of the same length, clean up one end of each, so that you can see the end grain. Straighten again if necessary.

Grain orientation.

Identify the reed and rift of the grain and put an ink dot on the end of the shaft as shown in Fig 8. Each time you spine a shaft, the dot will be at the top on the right hand of the tester. This is the stiffest orientation of the shaft. In Fig 8 below, the rift of the grain points to the nock, with the cock feather in the position shown. For a right handed archer, the rift points backward and if an arrow breaks in the bow (most unlikely but it has happened), the broken point will not be driven into the hand. For a left hander, simply fit the cock feather on the opposite side (think about it!).

Fig 8

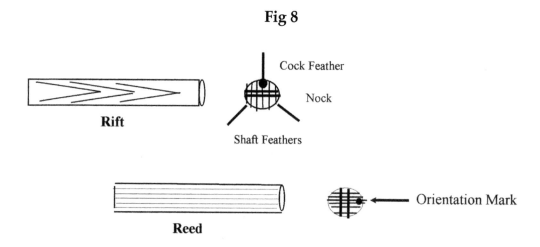

Set the spining length on your spine tester (see Fig 9). Mark it on your chart and then spine, weigh and record each shaft. Now you can start to make arrows!

Fig 9

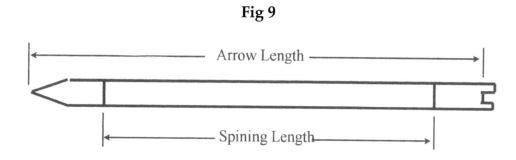

Some helpful tips on sanding.

Start with 40-grit paper on a cork faced block. You will be using this until you are within a few units of your final spine figure. Take a look at your chart. You will find a range of spines. The aim is to get them all to the spine of the highest existing shaft, taking into account the weight figures and remembering that sanding the end 4 to 5 inches of the shaft takes off weight with a small change in spine. Select a heavy and stiff shaft. Do 30 strokes with your sanding block *on each end*. Now spine and weigh the shaft. If you still need more weight off, repeat but with (say) 20 strokes. Spine and weight the shaft again. As you get nearer to your target, consider do you need weight off *and* higher spine? If so, again use less strokes but working from the middle to each end. Spine and weigh again. Is the weight OK but too stiff? If so, again use fewer strokes than before but over the centre 2/3 of the shaft, leaving then ends alone. Spine and weigh again. Repeat until OK then record and go on to the next shaft. In the notes on the spine tester, I did warn you that you would be doing a lot of spining and weighing! Another tip: after sanding, wipe off any excess sawdust adhering to the shaft, particularly when close to the final spine and weight.

Once you have all the shafts to the same spine, you must repeat the exercise to get all the shafts to 5 units "whippier", using the same techniques. Then repeat again to the next 5 units of spine. You can see that it is a slow process but it is the only way to keep weights and spines converging to a match.

When you are within 5 units or so of your final figure, you should fit the piles to your shafts. I use a router (I will detail the method and the jig later), but you can do it with a sharp knife and a safe-edge file. Be sure your piles are straight and true. You will probably find that the shaft is a greater diameter than the pile at the shoulder. I sand the shoulder back into the shaft in a taper for an inch or so, to blend shaft and pile neatly.

The pile must be fitted to the *opposite* end to your orientation mark because you need to preserve the orientation. Now you are going to shorten the shaft at the *nock* end. Before cutting the shaft, run a pencil line down the shaft, in line with your orientation mark for a couple of inches. Then cut your shaft to length and cut the taper for the nock. Before you do anything more, transfer your orientation mark back to the nock taper. You will need the orientation, as there is still some sanding to do to attain the final spine and weight. Put a nock on the shaft and run a pencil line round the shaft at the base of it. Now sand and blend this in until the pencil lines just disappear. You will have sanded out your shaft orientation but it is preserved on the nock taper. Remove the piles and nocks.

spine, weigh and record all your shafts again. Go back to sanding to get the final
es and weights but initially with 80 grit paper to final spine. Then with 180 grit
per, go 1 to 2 units further than your final spine. You will find that a coat or two of
Polyurethane, or whatever varnish you use, will stiffen up your shafts by 1 to 2 units.

A word of caution when sanding: as you sand a shaft it will warm up and warm timber is
less stiff than cold. When you get to the last part (with 80-grit paper and onward), leave
your shafts for at least 20 minutes before spining, to get accurate figures.

Fig 10 shows the workings for an actual set of arrows.

Fig 10

An actual set of arrows, 30" for 50lb bow.

Final spine to be 61 - 62. Original shafts: - 32", SP = 41- 45 @ 27", Wt = 450 - 458 grains

Arrow No		Col 1	Col 2	Col 3	Col 4	Col 5	Col 6	Bal
1	SP	53	55	56	60	63	61	13 $\frac{1}{4}$
	WT	410	390	368	359	350	450	
2	SP	51	55	56	60	63	62	13 $\frac{1}{4}$
	WT	412	394	372	360	350	448	
3	SP	52	55	56	60	63	62	13 $\frac{1}{8}$
	WT	420	393	371	360	350	448	
4	SP	53	55	55	60	63	62	13 $\frac{1}{8}$
	WT	416	393	377	356	350	447	
5	SP	55	55	56	60	63	61	13 $\frac{1}{4}$
	WT	408	396	378	357	352	450	
6	SP	56	56	56	60	63	61	13 $\frac{1}{4}$
	WT	412	395	371	360	352	451	
7	SP	50	55	56	60	63	61	13 $\frac{1}{8}$
	WT	418	390	372	358	350	447	
8	SP	50	55	56	60	63	61	13 $\frac{1}{8}$
	WT	424	390	370	360	352	447	

Column 1. All cut to 30", spined at 28 ½" (to allow for pile and nock). (The spine figure
increase from original is due to longer spine length). All sanded with 40 grit to column 2.

Column 2. Fit pile, cut to correct length, fit nock, blend nock/pile to shaft at each end, remove nock and pile, record new spine/weight in column 3

Column 3. Sand with 80 grit to column 4.

Column 4. Sand with 180 grit to column 5. Note, sand to 1-2 units whippier than final as seal coat will stiffen shaft by about 1 unit.

Column 5. Fit pile and nock permanently, remembering nock orientation. Seal (varnish) and fletch.

Column 6. Final spine, weight and point of balance. All well within spec of :-

+/- 1 G.N.A.S unit, +/- 5 grains, +/- ¼" balance point.

Notes on the above.

Arrows Nos. 5 & 6. Initial spine/weight (Col 1) 55/408 & 56/412. Sand 4-5 inches each end to reduce weight without spine change. Compare to: -

Arrows Nos. 7 & 8. Initial spine/weight 50/418 and 50/424. Sand (say) 30 strokes centre to each end, check spine/weight and continue to Col 2 figures.

General Notes.

1. You can match arrows for spine and weight. If you work carefully, taking the same amount off each end of your shafts, you will find that the point of balance will automatically be within spec. What you cannot do is to get all your shafts to exactly the same *diameter*, but the difference will be small and not worth worrying about.
2. When sanding shafts, position your shaft on the sanding board so that the section you want to work on is conveniently placed. Hold the shaft in one hand so that you can turn the shaft a small amount after each stroke and *count your sanding strokes*. Do one end and *immediately* repeat on the other end so that you do not forget. If you are sanding the centre, then of course, do it only once.
3. If you start with ¹¹/₃₂" shafts, then you will find that ⁵/₁₆" pile and nock will be correct. These will normally give you a short tapered length on the end of each arrow.
4. <u>Reinforcement</u>. Before finally fitting the pile, I like to drill down the shaft for about 1 ½" to 2", 1/8" diameter and glue in a length of 1/8" bamboo (kebab sticks are ideal). This gives that extra strength at the pile.

5. <u>Balance of arrows.</u> For good arrow flight, the point of balance should be about 3 to 7% in front of the centre (about $12^1/_2$" from the pile for a 28" arrow). These figures are not absolute but, generally speaking, a point of balance which is too far forward (say 15% to 20%) will make the pile drop and you will loose distance. If the point of balance is too far back, the arrow tends to climb which is ideal for flight and clout shooting but leads to inconsistency in target shooting. Your finished shafts, less pile, nock and fletching, should balance in the centre (except for chested shafts). The pile, being heavier than nock and fletching, will automatically bring the point of balance forward of centre.

Barrelled Arrows.

I would suggest that for your first attempt at barrelled arrows, you start with $^{11}/_{32}$" shafts and barrel down to $^9/_{32}$" at each end. To do this, you need to make yourself a template. Take a lath of timber about $^1/_8$" x 1" x the length of your arrow. You need to mark this out with arrow diameters at certain positions. Let us take a 28" arrow. We will leave the centre 4" at $^{11}/_{32}$". The rest of each end we will divide into 3. At these positions, we will mark the diameters that we want to achieve as in Fig 11.

Fig 11

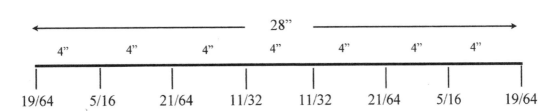

Note that the ends are $^{19}/_{64}$" not $^9/_{32}$". This gives us some spare to take off when fitting the pile and nock.

Clamp the template to the bench alongside your sanding board, and position your shaft so that the end corresponds to the end of your template.

Now with your small hand plane, start about 1" from the end taking short strokes while turning the shaft. Gradually lengthen the stroke, *always* going to the end of the shaft. A taper will materialise before your very eyes! Check continually with your hole jig, (see section on Tools) and when you are getting near, change to 40 grit paper on a block. It is unlikely that your taper will be even at your first attempt but by sanding off the high spots, you will get fairly close, though you will not achieve absolute accuracy. Now turn your shaft and do the other end.

You will of course have all your shafts in the rack. Do them all as above. Now spine and weight them and record on your work chart.

In this instance, we left a 4" section in the centre of the shaft the full $^{11}/_{32}$" diameter, and this, under normal circumstances, will allow you to make arrows down to about 60 spine at 28". If you think that your original shafts are not stiff enough to achieve the spine figure you are aiming for then make the centre section 6 or even 8 inches in length and mark your template accordingly. You can always get a whippier arrow by extending the taper into the 6 or 8 inch stiff section.

Arrows barrelled as above are ideal for target work, however, if you want to make clout or flight arrows, you can barrel them down to take ¼" piles and nocks. However, I would advise against using those for target work, as an arrow of that size hitting a target at an angle (as in a side wind) is much more likely to break.

By moving the stiff centre section 3" or 4" nearer the nock, you will make a "chested" arrow. Your template will be different of course, but the planing and sanding techniques are identical. The chested arrow compared to the barrelled arrow tends to fly a little higher, and may give you that extra yard or so. Since you are not looking for target style accuracy in your flight and clout arrows, fletch with small feathers (say 1 ¼" to 1 ½"), and trim them low to the shaft. A jig to cut feathers is described in the section on jigs.

Footed Arrows

In the introduction to this booklet, I promised that I would show you how to make footed arrows, and the time has now come.

There are a number of ways of making footed arrows, the simplest of which will be familiar to most archers. This consists of a footing (usually $^3/_8$ inch square in section) down the grain of which a 4 inch slot is sawn. The shaft is then planed to a 4 inch taper and glued into the footing forming a two point splice which makes a perfectly adequate footed arrow, with the added advantage that no jig is necessary for its' construction.

However, to produce footings of three and four points, together with an improved two-point footing, a jig is essential as is a table mounted router fitted with a fine height adjuster. The jig is shown in Fig 12 below.

Fig 12

It consists of a baseplate $^3/_8$ inch thick, of either good quality plywood or MDF, on the underside of which is fitted a strip which engages the mitre slot of the router table to control the movement of the jig on the table.

Also mounted on the baseplate is a slotted holder (shown in Fig 13) to carry the shaft/footing being machined. This in turn is attached to a further bar by means of two strips of plywood, one acting as a hinge, the other adjustable to enable the angle of the holder to be set. This assembly is positioned by a length of M6 screwed rod anchored to a block on the bar and held in place by two screwed wheels on either side of another block, which is fixed to the baseplate. The bar and holder are constrained to move across the baseplate by two $3/8$ by $1/8$ inch strips attached to the bar and running in grooves routed in the baseplate, thus allowing the depth of cut to be set. The two screwed wheels are about $1 1/2$ inches in diameter with an M6 nut set into the centre of each. The inner wheel is marked "0" and "1" on opposite sides to assist in setting the depth of cut.

Both the holder and the bar are made from $3/4$ inch MDF and the sliding assembly is prevented from lifting off the baseboard by an "L" sectioned block shown at the end of the baseplate. The other end of the baseplate is machined away to accommodate the indexing block.

Whilst dimensions are not critical, the length of the footing/shaft holder should be about 9 inches, to allow for the fitting of the toggle clamps etc. This is also a convenient length to hold a 14 inch length of footing material together with its' indexing block so that the footing can be machined on each end, since it is not possible to hold and index a single (say 6 inch) footing.

Also visible on the shaft side of the holder are two angled lines, the purpose of which will be explained later. Fig 13 shows the footing/shaft holder and an end view is shown in Fig 14.

Fig 13

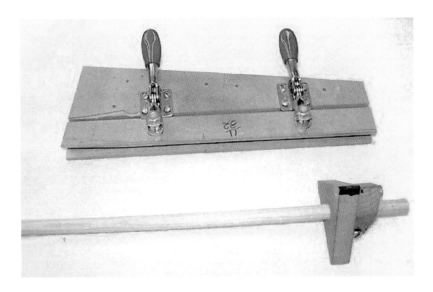

Fig 14

End view of footing/shaft holder

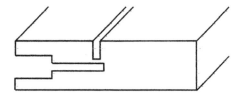

The slot, which carries the footing, is $^{11}/_{32}$ inches wide by $^{5}/_{16}$ inches deep and is further extended (by a tenon saw cut) by about another $^{3}/_{4}$ inches. A further slot is then machined in the top surface, to within about $^{1}/_{16}$ inch of the extended cut. This makes the top portion of the holder flexible enough to grip the shaft under the pressure of the two toggle clamps.

Fig 15 show the jig mounted on the router table, the router having a 60 degree cutter mounted in the collet and a footing with its indexing block in the holder. I will explain more about cutters and indexing later .

Fig 15

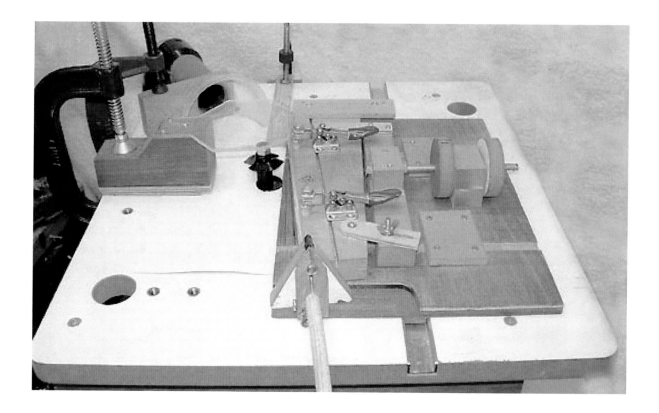

Also shown is the cutter shield of clear Perspex and the vacuum attachment to clear the chips. The red strip of wood clamped to the end of the table is there to align the baseplate. It is obvious that if the baseplate is placed on the table at the further end in the photograph and is then drawn to the near end, the cutter will foul the indexing block before it reaches the footing. The baseplate must be placed on the table in the position shown, and the coloured strip of wood assists in this placement.

It is essential when machining footings and shafts that the material is accurately indexed and this is accomplished by the use of a triangular indexing block for the three point footing and a square block for the two and four point footings.

Fig 16 shows both indexing blocks together with the method of clamping them to the shafts.

Fig 16

Both blocks should be accurately made with the mounting holes truly central. Cut the triangular block (from $3/8$ inch MDF) slightly oversize. Fit an $11/32$ inch shaft in the footing holder projecting over the machined away section of the baseplate. Drill an $11/32$ inch hole in the centre of the block and, sliding it on to the footing, offer it up to the machined baseplate section. It should be slightly oversize. Sand off the edge until it just fits.

Fit a block on to your disc sander at an *accurate* 60 degrees to the disc and using this, sand the other two edges of the block to fit.

The clamp is made of $3/8$ inch hardwood to the pattern shown. It is fixed to the block with its' hole in line with the index hole and is clamped to the shaft by an M4 screw and nut. The square block is made in the same fashion.

Clamp the indexing block to the footing in its holder, with whichever face puts the clamp screw in the most convenient place for tightening. Mark the top most corner of the block for identification and mark the square block similarly.

When you machine the footing you will make three cuts at one "depth of cut" setting, indexing between each. If you start with the marked corner uppermost, when that corner comes up again, it is time to increase the cut. This is the best way of checking on the progress of the operation.

Fig 17 shows a section of machined shafts and footings.

Fig 17

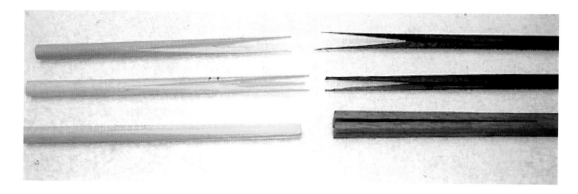

Notes.

1. Setting Up.

The following settings are for $^{11}/_{32}$ inch shafts. If you want to operate on other shaft sizes, you will have to make other interchangeable shaft holders.

To set the angle of the holder, set the hinge end of the holder on the edge of the baseplate, measure 4 inches along the holder and set that point to $^{11}/_{32}$ inch in from the edge of the baseplate, keeping the hinge end still on the baseplate edge. This will have set the holder at such an angle that it will produce a four-inch long joint. Cut a joint at this setting and, if you are satisfied with it, run an ink mark down the edge of the holder. If you later change the holder angle, you can subsequently return your original setting.

This setting will allow you to cut three point splices with the 60-degree cutter and two point splices with the 90-degree cutter. The makers are hopefully going to produce a 45-degree cutter, which will eventually allow the production of a four-point splice by this method. At the moment, the four-point splice is produced by a slightly different method.

It starts with a 6 inch footing of $^3/_8$ inch round or square section, with two cuts at right angles to each other down the footing for 4 inches. The four cuts in the shaft must be the same length *but only half the depth* so the holder angle must be changed to accommodate this. When you have it set correctly, mark it with a pen line as before.

The two-point footing is machined at the same holder angle setting as the three-point but using the four-sided index block and indexing 180 degrees instead of 90.

2. Cutters and Arbors.

These are available from the following:-

Wealden Tool Co.
2 Clinton Business Centre
Lodge Road
Staplehurst
Kent TN12 OQF
United Kingdom

Order Line 0800 328 4183
Technical Enquiries 01580 890500
sales@wealdentool.com

The cutters are from the "Mini Mould" series and the Arbors are 8 mm so you will also need an 8-mm collet for your router.

3. Shaft Orientation.

Mark the position of the cock feather on the *nock* end of your shaft and set each shaft into the holder such that the first cut is in line with the cock feather. Not *strictly* necessary, but it does produce a better looking set of arrows!

4. Cutter Depth Setting.

Initially, bring the shaft just into contact with the cutter. One turn of the depth setting wheel will advance the cut by one millimetre. For softwood shafts, you can usually get away with 2 mm cuts for the first two cuts, subsequently 1 mm, and at the end $^1/_2$ mm. For hardwood footings, use 1 mm and $^1/_2$ mm. These settings have worked for me!

5. Router Speed.

With these cutters and the extended arbor, I tend to get slight vibration on my router. Reducing the router speed completely cures this problem with no loss of cutter efficiency.

6. Assembly of 2 and 3 point footings.

You will need:-

1. Waterproof glue. *Not PVA.* I use "Titebond", available from Axminster Power Tool Co.
2. Strips of rubber cut from an old inner tube, and about $3/8''$ wide, 12 – 13" long.

Take a footing, and wrap *tightly* 3 – 4 turns of rubber strip just below the base of the cuts. Tuck the end through the last loop and pull tight. Apply glue to the cuts in both the footing and shaft, mate them up, wrap with the rubber band and finish off by tucking the end through the last turn. A final tap on the end of the footing will ensure proper seating. Concentricity of shaft and footing is assured by the method of cutting.

7. Assembly of 4 point footings.

Note that this operation will become redundant, when and if a 45-degree cutter becomes available. Take a footing, and wrap *tightly* 3 – 4 turns of rubber strip just below the base of the cuts. Tuck the end through the last loop and pull tight. Hold the footing in the vice *tightly*, and slide a piece of 60 – 80 grit paper up and down each inside corner to round it off. Push a cocktail stick through each cut in the footing, about 1" above the base. This will open out the cuts. Now, put a line of glue in each flute of the shaft, and enter it into the footing to the sticks. Remove the sticks, and tap the shaft home with a block of wood. You will both feel and hear when it is fully home. Now bind the whole footing tightly with the rubber strip, tucking the end through the last loop. Remove from the vice and make sure that the footing is on straight. I do this by rolling the shaft along the bench with the footing overhanging. When you are sure it is on straight, *give a final tap to make sure it is fully home* and return the shaft to the rack. Repeat for the rest of your shafts. When the glue is set (I leave mine for 24 hours) remove the wrappings and again check for straightness. If they are out of true at all, it should only be by a very small margin. You are now going to plane down the flat sides of the footings to the size of the shafts. Take care to keep them true. Now also is the time to take account of any small inaccuracies, which you may have found, after removing the bindings. Having got the four sides flat and true, set them corner ways in your grooved plank and plane off the corners to give an octagon, with eight sides as equal as you can get them. You now have eight corners; plane these down and your footing will be almost round. Now drive it, shaft first, through consecutively smaller holes down to $11/32''$ in your dowel plate and you have a footed shaft of about $11/32''$ diameter. Between driving through consecutive holes in the dowel plate, sand off most of the excess timber. This will make the job easier. You can now proceed to sand, spine and weigh as for self arrows.

If you want barrelled arrows, sand down to 10 units stiffer than the final spine. Now machine to take $^9/_{32}$" piles, cut to length, and taper for $^9/_{32}$ nocks. Now you have to taper both pile and nock end to blend in nock and pile, making your tapers 5 – 6 " long and spining and weighing as you go. Take it easy. Do all your shafts 3 to 4 units at a time, until you get to within 4 to 5 units of final spine. Then, as for self arrows, reduce to final spine with fine paper. You will find that the initial 5 –6" tapers on nock and pile end of your shaft will change the weight considerably, but will not change the spine by more than a few units.

Footed, and particularly footed and barrelled arrows, while not inherently more difficult to make, do demand more care and attention to detail. I would recommend that you make a few sets of self arrows before tackling footed ones!

8. With all the footings fitted, you can go back to making arrows.

The Balance

Fig 18 shows the completed balance and Fig 19 is a close up of the beam showing the planes in detail.

Fig 18

Fig 19

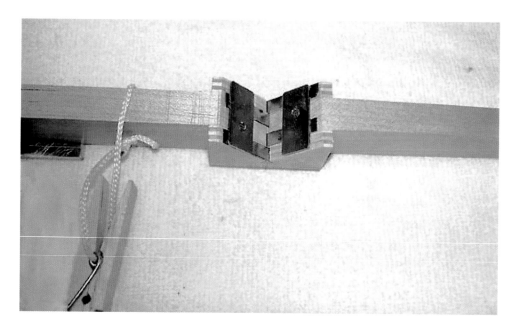

To make the balance, you will need a piece of hardwood 1 inch x ½ inch and at least 30 inches long, with two side cheeks 1 ½ x 1 x ¼ inch glued in the positions shown in Fig 20 below.

Fig 20

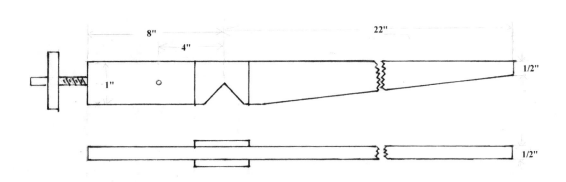

The "V" is cut with a fine tooth saw (preferably a band saw), with the cuts being extended by about $1/8$ inch as shown in Fig 21a. Be sure that the cuts are square across the beam. These cuts and faces carry the metal strips, which form the planes, which in turn support the beam on the knife-edge. The accuracy and sensitivity of your balance will depend on the accurate cutting and fitting of these planes.

The planes are made from a junior hacksaw blade. Grind the teeth off the blade, grinding far enough back to remove the wavy edge, which gives the teeth their set. Then, on an oilstone, polish one end of the blade for a length of about ¼ inch. Break off 1 inch of that end of the blade. Repeat three times and you will have four planes $1/8$ to $3/16$ inch wide x 1 inch long with one end polished.

You now need two clamps to hold the planes in place. These need to be ¾ x $3/8$ inch and about 1/16 inch thick with a countersunk hole in the middle to take a $3/8$ inch No 4 screw. The clamps can be of wood or metal. Set the planes in the beam, sliding them down into the extended saw cuts as shown in Figs 21a and 21b with the clamps holding them in place. You could of course, fix the planes in position with adhesive (epoxy or similar), but be sure that you keep any adhesive well away from the polished faces and that the planes lay flat to the wood.

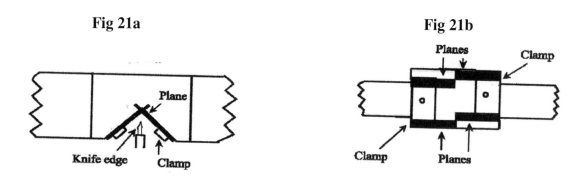

Fig 21a

Fig 21b

Scribe a line across the beam *exactly* over the knife-edge. From this line, measure 4 inches towards the butt end of the beam. Square a line down the beam at this point and drill a $^1/_8$ inch hole in the centre of the beam. This hole will carry, on a loop of string, an old-fashioned spring clothes peg, with two "Vs" filed in its mating faces to hold the arrow being weighed.

Into the butt end of the beam, fix a 4 inch length of M6 screwed rod with epoxy adhesive. This will carry a wheel of hardwood about $2^1/_2$ to 3 inches in diameter by about $^1/_2$ inch thick. With an M6 nut fixed into the centre of the wheel, this will be used as a fine adjustment to balance the beam.

You will now need a scale as shown in Fig 22. Draw it out *accurately* on paper. Make it 500 mm long divided into CMS. These are further sub-divided into 2mm divisions. Mark each 100 division in red for ease of reading. The 2mm divisions will equal 2 grains in weight. The scale must be glued to the side of the beam so that the zero point coincides exactly with the knife-edge. You will have to discard the first 2 to 3 cms of the scale because of the wooden shoulders of the beam. This will enable you to weigh arrows up to 500 grains and also to weigh piles down to about 20 grains. (437.5 grains = 1 oz = 28.4 grams).

You can also make the scale from a dressmaker's tape calibrated in cms.

Fig 22

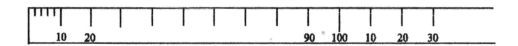

You now need to set the balance on a baseboard. Use either hardwood or MDF. 18 x 2 x $^1/_2$ inch is about right but the size is not critical. The knife-edge is the blade of a Stanley knife set into a saw cut in the edge of a piece of ¼ inch hardwood. This should be mounted on the baseboard, 3 inches from the end so that in use, the baseboard can be set on a table with the clothes peg over-hanging the table edge. At the other end of the baseboard, arrange the two stops to limit the beam movement to ¼ inch above and below level.

You now have some delicate work ahead in balancing the bare beam. Set the zeroing disc central on the screwed rod. Fit the clothes peg to the beam on its loop of string and place the beam on the knife-edge. Initially it will not balance because the long end of the beam will be too heavy. You will have to add weight to the other end of the beam. In my case, a piece of $^1/_8$ inch thick brass, 2 ½ x 1 inch, mounted with two screws on the butt end of the beam, was sufficient. Initially it was slightly heavy but judicious use of a file finally produced a balance. A time consuming job but I have yet to find a better method. If the weight is only slightly heavy, and the mounting holes are slotted, try moving it nearer the centre.

Make a cursor as shown in Fig 23a and b. The platform is of hardwood, just wide enough to slide easily on the beam. The two sides are of clear plastic with a line scribed down the centre of one piece. If you make your cursor $1^1/_8$ inches long it should be too heavy.

Fig 23a   **Fig 23b**

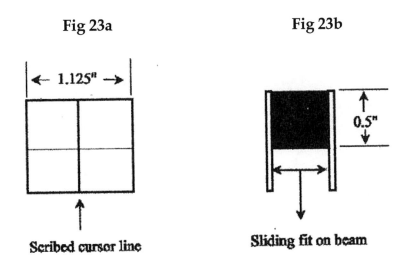

Scribed cursor line   Sliding fit on beam

Calibration.

You need a known weight to calibrate your balance. I used a 20 gram weight which is 308 grains. With your balance set up and in balance without the cursor, place your known weight in the clothes peg. Then slide the cursor along the beam until you have balance. It should read *less* than the correct weight. Now adjust the weight of the cursor until the calibration is correct. Your balance is now ready to use.

Some notes on the use of your balance.

1. The balance of the beam will vary with a) temperature and b) humidity. Therefore, *always* check the balance of the bare beam and adjust with the wheel if necessary, before doing a series of weighings.

2. Your balance may not be absolutely accurate but readings will be repeatable so you can compare arrow weights accurately.

3. If you make another weight, exactly the same weight as your cursor and use them both together, one on top of the other, you will get half the weight readings. I.e. 20 grams will weigh 154 grains instead of 308 grains. In this way, you can weigh arrows up to 1000 grains. Alternatively, you can mount another clothes peg two inches from the knife-edge. This will allow you to weigh arrows, which are heavier than 500 grains with the same cursor. Think about it!

The Spine Tester

The completed spine tester is shown in Fig 24.

Fig 24

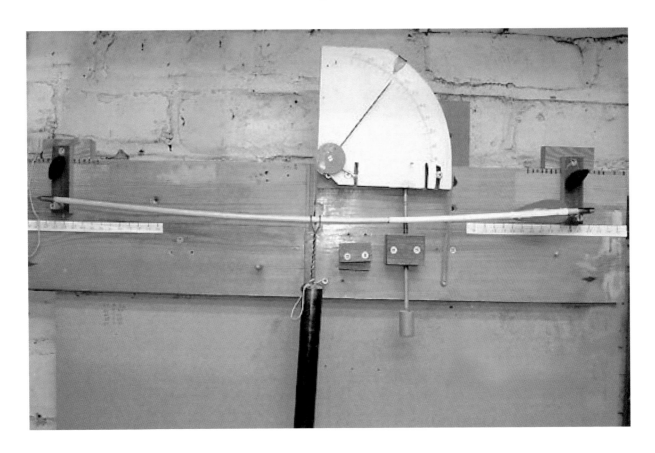

Start by making the measuring section of the instrument (Fig 25). You will need a quarter circle of ½" plywood or M.D.F. with a radius of 7". Cover this with white card, on which to mark your scale.

Fig 25

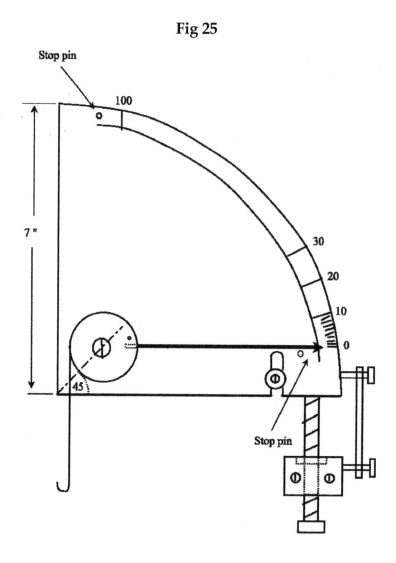

You now need a 1 ½" diameter wheel, ¼" thick (Fig 26), with a groove around its' circumference to take a thin cord which carries a hook on which the arrow rests. A thin rod about 4" long with one end pointed is glued into a hole in the wheel edge to form a pointer of about 5" long. Just above the pointer, and on the face side of the wheel, drill a small hole through to the groove on the wheel edge. You can feed the cord through this hole and secure it by means of a small tapered stick pushed into the hole to wedge the cord in place. This will give some adjustment of the position of the hook. Alternatively, in place of the cord, a length of leader tape from an old audio cassette may be used. This will hold the hook in the correct orientation.

Fig 26

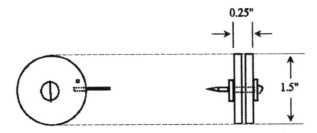

Now you need to find a screw on which the wheel will revolve. A No 4 x ¾" Roundhead will be ideal. Drill the centre of the wheel with a neat clearance hole so that the wheel revolves smoothly on the screw. Mount the wheel as shown in Fig 25, on a line, which bisects the right angle, using a small washer between the wheel and the board to ensure smooth running. Also shown in the figure is a hole for a screw with which to mount the quadrant on the baseboard, together with a curved slot to take another screw with a washer. This mounting allows the quadrant to pivot to accommodate adjustment of the zero point. The adjustment is made with a screwed rod pressing upward onto the bottom of the quadrant, which is kept in contact with the adjuster by means of a rubber band.

Now make the baseboard. For this you will need a piece of timber or ¾" M.D.F., about 6" x 1" dressed, and 30" long (Fig 27a). On this, at the top and to the right of centre you need to fix another piece 8" x 1 ½" x ½" as a spacer. This will ensure that when the quadrant is fitted on the spacer, with its' cord and hook on the centre line of the baseboard, there will be enough clearance for the feathers not to foul the baseboard.

Fig 27a   **Fig 27b**

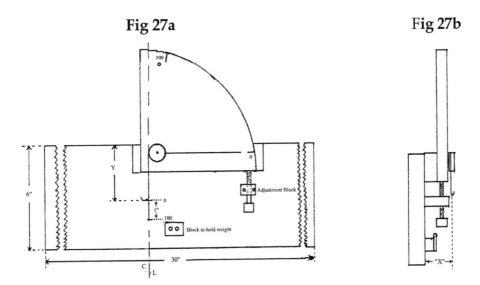

Fit the quadrant to the spacer on its pivot screw and also fit the retaining screw and washer. With the bottom of the quadrant level, put the retaining screw about half way along the slot, so ensuring adjustment in both directions.

Make the adjustment block by sinking a small nut into a block of wood, with a clearance hole through the block so that a length of screwed rod with a knob on the bottom, may be used to adjust the height of the quadrant. M6 nuts and rod are ideal (Figs 25, 27a and 28). A rubber band attached to the quadrant and baseboard will keep the quadrant in contact with the screw.

Fig 28

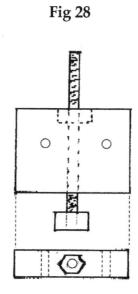

You can now calibrate the measuring quadrant (Fig 27a). With a small set square, held against the hook and the baseboard, pull the hook down a little so that the pointer is raised approximately 1/8" above the stop pin. Mark the baseboard at the level of the hook and the quadrant at the end of the pointer. This is your zero position. Now from the baseboard zero make a mark exactly 1" below. With the square still against the hook, pull down to the 1" mark and again mark the scale at the end of the pointer. This is your 100 mark. Divide your scale into 10, and then each division into another 10, and you will have a scale easily readable to 1/100" (1 g.n.a.s. unit).

Only two more jobs to complete your tester! You need a 1½ lb. weight. Mine is a 7" length of 1" diameter steel bar, with a length of stiff wire attached in the form of a double hook (Fig 29). The bar is filed until it weights exactly 1 ½ lbs on a 5 lb. Kitchen scale. A tip here, when you get your piece of steel bar, get about 7 ½" of it. Measure the length and weigh the bar. You can then calculate how much to take off. Remove a little less than this amount and then file to the correct weight. You also need some sort of a hook on which to hang your weight when it is not on the arrow (Fig 27a).

Fig 29

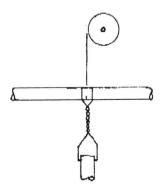

The last job! Make two supports for the arrow, adjustable so that you can spine arrows of varying lengths. First make the arrow supports. Saw a slot down a length of ¼" dowel with a junior hacksaw to a depth of about ¾". Break off about ½" length of junior hacksaw blade and "Araldite" this into the dowel slot, teeth down, as shown in Fig 30a, leaving 1/8" above the dowel. When the adhesive is set, file a "V" into the blade (Fig 30b). This will locate your arrow, and must be set at the distance "X" (Fig 30b). Needless to say, you need two of these.

Fig 30a   **Fig 30b**

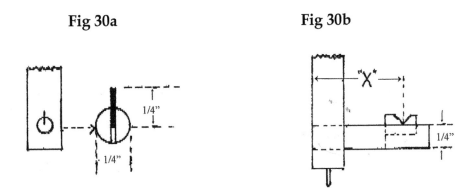

The two carriers need to be ½" x 3/8" hardwood, length equal to dimension "Y" plus ½" (Fig 27a). The top hook section can be made up of any ¼" thick material, glued and pinned so that they are a nice sliding fit on top of the baseboard. The ¼" hole to take the arrow support should be drilled at dimension "Y" plus ¼", so that the supporting blade shall be level with the hook (Fig 31a). Now drive a small panel pin into the bottom of each carrier to act as a pointer for the scales you will make.

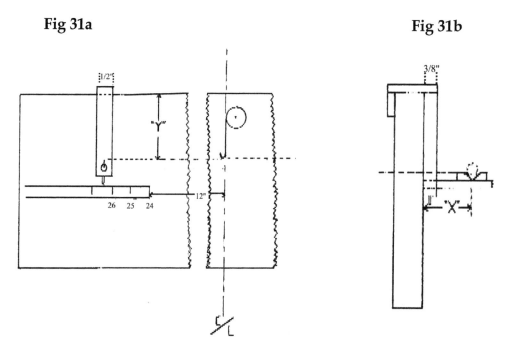

Fig 31a   Fig 31b

Take two pieces of ½″ card and mark them with arrow lengths as shown (Fig 31a) I.e. 24, 25, 26 etc, remembering that 1″ difference in arrow length is ½″ each end so that your 1″ scale marks are only 1/2″ apart. Remember also to make right and left hand scales. Now stick them to the baseboard, one each side, with the 24″ marks exactly 12″ from the centre line.

If you have got this far, you now have an accurate spine tester. You will find, when you make a set of arrows, you will spine and weigh each arrow some 50 to 60 times.

Some notes on using your spine tester.

3. You need to identify the "reed" and "rift" in the grain of your dowels. See Fig 32.

Fig 32

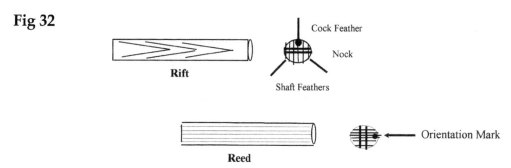

Always place the arrow on the spine tester with the "reed" of the grain vertical (Fig 33)

42

Fig 33

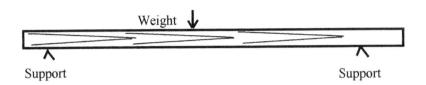

2. Spining length. The arrow must be supported at the base of the knock, and the shoulder of the pile. The spining length will therefore be less than the arrow length by the length of the knock plus pile.

3. Place the weight *gently* on the shaft! A 1 ½ lb. Weight dropped onto a shaft may well break it.

4. When initially sorting rough dowels for spine and weight, *always* spine at the same length. You can then add to your stock at any time, safe in the knowledge that all your spine measurements are at the same length. I use 27″.

5. The spine number of an $^{11}/_{32}$″ diameter redwood dowel will increase approximately by five units per inch. I.e. 50 @ 27″, 55 @ 28″, 60 @ 29″ etc.

It is a good idea to mount both spine tester and balance solidly. Mine are mounted on a piece of ½″ M.D.F. 30″ wide x 24″ deep, the spine tester on top. This board is in turn screwed to the wall with the spine tester at head height. It can be removed and mounted on feet so that it can be used on a table or bench. Both instruments, but most particularly the balance, should be level in both horizontal planes when in use.

Addendum:

If you make a weight of ¾lb it will halve the spine reading of any arrow. This is very useful if you are making light arrows to match small bows of 12 – 20 lbs draw weight. Arrows of spine ratings of, say, 90 will almost certainly be permanently bent or possibly broken if tested on a spine tester under 1 ½ lb weight especially if they are more than 24″ long.

Nocks and Feathers

Nocks

I admit that I am lazy! I use plastic nocks on my arrows. They are strong with slots of exactly the same size, and easily replaced when damaged. I use a sanding disc and a jig to cut the necessary taper to take the nock (see Jigs). I find this method produces a better finish and is quicker than the "pencil sharpener" types. How long does it take to grind nock tapers on shafts? – Ten to fifteen minutes.

If you want to make the traditional self nocks, I strongly suggest that you fit nock inserts to your shafts. Horn is the traditional material but I have used wood. Ebony is good and other hardwoods are equally suitable. If you make footed arrows, a nock insert of the footing timber looks well.

Your insert must be fitted *with* the grain of the timber so that the nock is cut *across* the grain. (See the spine tester for an explanation of reed and rift). Saw a tapered slot down the end of your arrow, about 1" long. Originally I made a jig for this but sawing freehand is not difficult. Practice on scrap dowels! Saw or sand a matching taper on your insert *and make it a good fit*. Glue it in and when the glue is set, cut the nock. Hacksaw blades taped together make a good tool – that way, all your nocks will be the same size. Don't forget to round off the base of the nock, and make all smooth with fine abrasive paper.

The one problem with self nocks is, if you break one it usually means a lost arrow.

Feathers

As with nocks, I use ready cut feathers. I shoot 28" arrows, and my preference is for 4" feathers for my target arrows.

Generally speaking I would recommend the following:-

> 2" to 2 ½" for 24" to 26" arrows.
> 3" for 27" to 28" arrows.
> 4" for over 28" arrows.

Of course it is a matter of personal choice, but remember the larger the feather, the slower your shaft, which is probably better for short range, (indoor)? Shooting – the arrows tend to straighten up faster.

For your clout and flight arrows, where distance is relatively more important than accuracy, then a smaller feather is appropriate. For my clout arrows (28" long), I use feathers 1 ¾" long and ½" high. Providing the arrows are well matched, these sizes are plenty big enough. I make mine by cutting down standard 3" feathers, using the tool described in the chapter on Jigs.

You can of course glue your feathers onto the arrow and shape them with a feather burner, which is only a shaped piece of fire element wire heated by current from a low voltage transformer, but a word of warning! *Burning feathers stink*. So, in the interests of domestic harmony, *don't do it in the house*, and be careful as the primary side of your transformer is at *mains* voltage, and *must* be adequately shielded.

Tools

1. Band-saw

Not absolutely essential but it does make life easier, especially when cutting timber into $3/8''$ sticks. My saw is a small, 2 wheel "Delta" machine.

2. Router.

If you only want to make self arrows, you can mange without one, although it does make the job of fitting piles easier. It is essential if you propose to make footed arrows with a four point splice. Again, jigs will be described later. The machine *must* have fine height adjustment.

3. Sander

Either disc or belt will do. The disc sander with adjustable table, incorporating a mitre guide is useful. I use mine to sand shafts to take nocks and tapered fit piles. It is much better than pencil sharpening types. Again, jigs will be detailed later.

4. Pillar drill.

Alternatively a pistol drill mounted in a drill stand. Small, bench mounted drills are so cheap these days that it is worth buying one for the convenience of not having to set the pistol drill in it's stand each time.

5. Rounding plane.

You can round off your shafts with a small, sharp hand plane if you work carefully, and if you are not making a lot of arrows, but a rounding plane will round your shafts, all to the same size, with a lot less work. Mine has a $1/2''$ entry bush and produces $11/32''$ dowels from $3/8''$ square sticks. You will lose 4" to $4^1/2''$ of timber from each piece, so allow for this in your wood. If you make a holder for your sticks, to fit in the chuck of your drill, and clamp the drill horizontally in a bench stand, then, with the drill running, you can feed the rounder down the stick to produce a dowel. A variable speed drill, with a foot switch to leave both hands free, and a speed of 400 rpm is ideal.

The makers of the rounding plane are:-

Ashem Crafts
2 Oakleigh Avenue
Hallow
Worcestershire
WR2 6NG
Tel 01905 640070
enquiries@ashemcrafts.com

6. Sanding blocks

I have three, armed with 40, 80 and 180 grit paper.

7. Small hand plane

With an adjustable mouth. Keep it sharp!

8. Sanding Board.

A piece of ½" to $^5/_8$" x 6" timber about 3 feet long. Groove 90 degrees x ¼" deep on one edge to hold shafts for sanding.

Jigs

1. Dowel Plate and Hole Size Jig

Obtain a piece of steel bar 9″ x 1″ x $^1/_8$″. Gauge plate is best but if you cannot get this, *bright* mild steel bar is acceptable.

This must be drilled with a series of holes, starting ¼″ diameter at one end, and progressing to ½″ at the other, each hole $^1/_{64}$″ larger than the last. Clamp the steel when drilling it, and use a drilling machine if possible, together with *sharp*, high-speed steel drills. The holes need to be true circles with sharp edges. They should be counter sunk on one side to within $^1/_{64}$″ of the face, and the face side should be stoned on an oil stone to give clean sharp edges to the holes.

Now drill a piece of hardwood with a corresponding set of holes, and mount the dowel plate on it with the plate holes misplaced to the next size hole up; i.e. the ¼″ hole will be over the $^{17}/_{64}$″ hole in the wood and so on. If you drill and counter sink mounting holes in the dowel plate and mount it on the hardwood, you can drill the timber and then move the dowel plate up one hole.

The dowel plate can now be held in the vice so that you can drive dowels through with a mallet.

The hole size jig has the same series of holes drilled in a piece of 9″x1″x1″ thick M.D.F., the hole sizes being marked so that they are easy to read.

2. Nock and Pile Taper Grinding Jig

This jig is designed to produce the tapered end of the shaft to take the nock, and with a different guide block, the taper to take a taper-fitting pile (Fig 34a and b).

A sander is necessary, either disc or belt. The table is fitted with either the nock or pile guide block. In operation, the shaft is fed to the disc or belt. While being kept against the guide block and turned in the fingers.

See also the pile fitting jig.

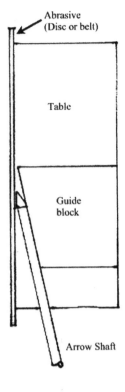

Fig 34a

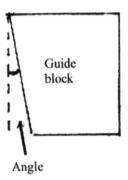

Fig 34b

Angle

12 $\frac{1}{2}$ deg for nock
6 $\frac{1}{4}$ deg for pile

3. Pile Fitting Jig.

This is simply a length of ½" x 1 ½" timber about 6" to 8" long, with a 90 degree groove
$\frac{1}{8}$" or so deep routed down the centre of one face. Mounted over this at one end, is
another piece of ½" x 1 ½" timber 3" long, with a piece of leather glued to it, and held in
position with rubber bands (see Fig 35). The arrow shaft is pushed through the groove
and rotated, being fed over a bottom cutting router bit to a stop on the fence (Fig 36). In
this way a parallel spigot is formed, of the correct length and diameter to fit the pile. The
technique is, withdraw the router cutter below the shaft, advance till it touches the shaft
and form a short spigot. Withdraw the shaft and test the fit in the pile. Advance the cutter
slightly and make another cut. When the diameter is correct take the full length cut on the
shaft. I like to leave the spigot a tight fit from the cutter, and finish with a safe edge file.

Of course you need a fine height adjuster on your router.

Fig 35

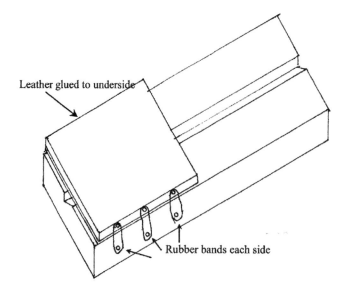

Leather glued to underside

Rubber bands each side

Fig 36

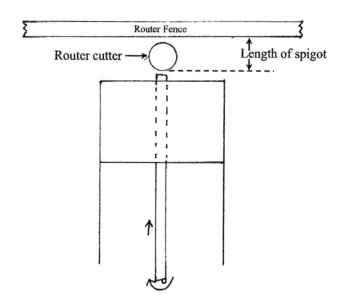

Router Fence

Router cutter →

Length of spigot

If another pile fitting jig is constructed with a 4 degree tapered wedge fitted to its' base (see photographs in Fig 37), shafts can be machined to provide a shoulder for the taper fitting pile to mate up to. This makes a much stronger and tidier pile fitting.

Fig 37

4. The Feather Cutting Jig

This jig (Fig 38) is designed to cut feathers to shape with a curved bladed craft knife. The feather is clamped between the jig and the shaped template, and can be cut by a rocking motion of the curved blade. By this means the feather is cut by pressure on the blade, rather than by dragging the blade over the vane, which invariably results in a misshapen vane.

I only use this jig to produce small feathers for flight/clout arrows, and I normally cut them from a standard feather of appropriate size. I use this in preference to the feather burner. It is just as accurate and of course does *not* create the smell of burning feathers. Obviously, design your own templates. I make mine of $^1/_{16}$" ply.

Fig 38

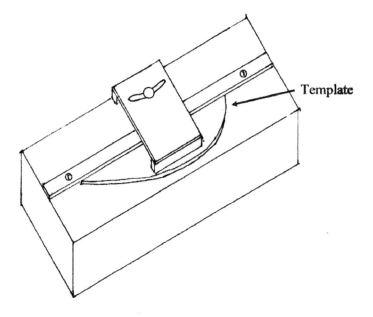

Template

Acknowledgements

My thanks to all who have helped in any way in the production of this book, particularly my son-in-law, Ian Pegg, and Stan Atkinson who inveigled me into writing it in the first place.

Bill Searle

The author at work

Made in the USA
San Bernardino, CA
08 January 2013